CONTENTS

INTRODUCTION

Pancreatitis is inflammation of the pancreas and may be acute or chronic. Acute pancreatitis is acute inflammation of the pancreas and a common cause of acute abdominal pain causing hospitalisation. In the majority of patients, the illness settles over a few days but in 25% of cases it is more severe and associated with organ failure or pancreatic necrosis, requiring critical care and a prolonged hospital stay. The incidence in the UK is approximately 56 cases per 100,000 people per year and the overall mortality rate around 5%. In some cases acute pancreatitis may progress to chronic pancreatitis, particularly after recurrent attacks. Chronic pancreatitis is an inflammatory process of the pancreas that results in fibrosis, cyst formation and stricturing of the pancreatic duct. It usually presents with chronic abdominal pain but the clinical course is variable. The annual incidence in Western Europe is about 5 new cases per 100,000 people, although this is probably an underestimate. Most people with chronic pancreatitis have had 1 or more attacks of acute pancreatitis. In others, chronic pancreatitis has a more insidious onset and delay in diagnosis is common.

In the UK approximately 50% of cases of acute pancreatitis are caused by gallstones, 25% by alcohol and 25% by other factors. Alcohol is responsible for 70–80% of cases of chronic pancreatitis and cigarette smoking is strongly associated with chronic pancreatitis; and is thought to exacerbate the condition. Acute and chronic pancreatitis may be idiopathic or, in about 5% of cases, caused by hereditary factors (in these cases there is usually a positive family history). Other causes include hypercalcaemia, hyperlipidaemia or autoimmune disease. In acute and chronic pancreatitis identifying the cause may not be straightforward and specialist investigations may be necessary. Management of acute pancreatitis in the early stages is supportive. Intravenous fluid replacement has an important role but the type and rate of administration of the fluid is unclear. The role of antibiotics in preventing infection is hotly debated. It is recognised that patients who develop infected pancreatic necrosis should undergo a form of drainage or necrosectomy to treat this but the type of intervention for each patient is unclear. Indications for referral to a specialist pancreatic centre are variable and require clarification.

PANCREATITIS

Pancreatitis is a disease in which your pancreas becomes inflamed. The pancreas is a large gland behind your stomach and next to your small intestine. Your pancreas does two main things:

• It releases powerful digestive enzymes into your small intestine to help you digest food.

• It releases insulin and glucagon into your bloodstream. These hormones help your body control how it uses food for energy.

Your pancreas can be damaged when digestive enzymes begin working before your pancreas releases them.

Types of Pancreatitis

The two forms of pancreatitis are acute and chronic.

Acute pancreatitis is sudden inflammation that lasts a short time. It can range from mild discomfort to a severe, life-threatening illness. Most people with acute pancreatitis recover completely after getting the right treatment. In severe cases, acute pancreatitis can cause bleeding, serious tissue damage, infection, and cysts. Severe pancreatitis can also harm other vital organs such as the heart, lungs, and kidneys.

Chronic pancreatitis is long-lasting inflammation. It most often happens after an episode of acute pancreatitis. Another top cause is drinking lots of alcohol for a long period of time. Damage to your pancreas from heavy alcohol use may not cause symptoms for many years, but then you may suddenly have severe pancreatitis symptoms.

Pancreatitis Symptoms

Symptoms of acute pancreatitis

• Fever

• Higher heart rate

• Nausea and vomiting

• Swollen and tender belly

• Pain in the upper part of your belly that goes into your back. Eating may make it worse, especially foods high in fat.

Symptoms of chronic pancreatitis

The symptoms of chronic pancreatitis are similar to those of acute pancreatitis. But you may also have:

• Constant pain in your upper belly that radiates to your back. This pain may be disabling.

• Diarrhea and weight loss because your pancreas isn't releasing enough enzymes to break down food

• Upset stomach and vomiting

Pancreatitis Causes and Risk Factors

Acute pancreatitis causes include:

• Autoimmune diseases

• Drinking lots of alcohol

• Infections

• Gallstones

• Medications

• Metabolic disorders

• Surgery

• Trauma

In up to 15% of people with acute pancreatitis, the cause is unknown.

Chronic pancreatitis causes include:

• Cystic fibrosis

• Family history of pancreas disorders

• Gallstones

• High triglycerides

• Longtime alcohol use

• Medications

In about 20% to 30% of cases, the cause of chronic pancreatitis is unknown. People with chronic pancreatitis are usually men between ages 30 and 40.

Pancreatitis Complications

Pancreatitis can have severe complications, including:

• Diabetes if there's damage to the cells that produce insulin

• Infection of your pancreas

• Kidney failure

• Malnutrition if your body can't get enough nutrients from the food you eat because of a lack of digestive enzymes

Pancreatic cancer

• Pancreatic necrosis, when tissues die because your pancreas isn't getting enough blood

• Problems with your breathing when chemical changes in your body affect your lungs. Pseudocysts, when fluid collects in pockets on your pancreas. They can burst and become infected.

Pancreatitis Diagnosis

To diagnose acute pancreatitis, your doctor tests your blood to measure two digestive enzymes: amylase and lipase. High levels of these two enzymes mean you probably have acute pancreatitis. Other tests can include:

Pancreatic function test to find out whether your pancreas is making the right amounts of digestive enzymes

• Ultrasound, CT scan, and MRI, which make images of your pancreas

• ERCP, in which your doctor uses a long tube with a camera on the end to look at your pancreatic and bile ducts

• Biopsy, in which your doctor uses a needle to remove a small piece of tissue from your pancreas to be studied

In some cases, your doctor may test your blood and poop to confirm the diagnosis. They may also do a glucose tolerance test to measure damage to the cells in your pancreas that make insulin.

Pancreatitis Treatment

Treatment for acute pancreatitis

You'll probably need to stay in the hospital, where your treatment may include:

• Antibiotics if your pancreas is infected

• Intravenous (IV) fluids, given through a needle

• Low-fat diet or fasting. You might need to stop eating so your pancreas can recover. In this case, you'll get nutrition through a feeding tube.

• Pain medicine

If your case is more severe, your treatment might include:

• ERCP to take out gallstones if they're blocking your bile or pancreatic ducts

• Gallbladder surgery if gallstones caused your pancreatitis

• Pancreas surgery to clean out fluid or dead or diseased tissue

Treatment for chronic pancreatitis

If you have chronic pancreatitis, you might need more treatments, including:

• Insulin to treat diabetes

• Pain medicine

• Pancreatic enzymes to help your body get enough nutrients from your food

• Surgery or procedures to relieve pain, help with drainage, or treat blockages

Pancreatitis Prevention

Because many cases of pancreatitis are caused by alcohol abuse, prevention often focuses on limiting how much you drink or not drinking at all. If your drinking is a concern, talk to your doctor or health care professional about an alcohol treatment center. A support group such as Alcoholics Anonymous could also help.

Stop smoking, follow your doctor's and dietitian's advice about your diet, and take your medications so you'll have fewer and milder attacks of pancreatitis.

PANCREATITIS DIET

What foods should you eat

Pancreatitis is a serious condition that occurs when the pancreas becomes inflamed. The pancreas is an organ that produces insulin and digestive enzymes. The same enzymes that help with digestion can sometimes injure the pancreas and cause irritation. This irritation can be short-term or long-term.

Certain foods may make abdominal pain caused by pancreatitis worse. It is important to choose foods that will not make symptoms worse and cause discomfort while recovering from pancreatitis.

Best foods to eat for pancreatitis

Beans and lentils may be recommended for a pancreatitis diet because of their high fiber content. The first treatment for pancreatitis sometimes requires a person to refrain from consuming all food and liquids for several hours or even days. Some people may need an alternate way of getting nutrition if they are unable to consume the required amounts for their body to work properly. When a doctor allows a person to eat again, they will likely recommend that a person eats small meals frequently throughout the day and avoids fast food, fried foods, and highly processed foods.

Here is a list of foods that may be recommended and why:

• vegetables

• beans and lentils

• fruits

• whole grains

• other plant-based foods that are not fried

These foods are recommended for people with pancreatitis because they tend to be naturally low in fat, which eases the amount of work the pancreas needs to do to aid digestion.

Fruits, vegetables, beans, lentils, and whole grains are also beneficial because of their fiber content. Eating more fiber can lower the chances of having gallstones or elevated levels of fats in the blood called triglycerides. Both of those conditions are common causes of acute pancreatitis. In addition to fiber, the foods listed above also provide antioxidants. Pancreatitis is an inflammatory condition, and antioxidants may help reduce inflammation.

Lean meats

Lean meats can help people with pancreatitis meet their protein needs.

Medium-chain triglycerides (MCTs)

For people with chronic pancreatitis, adding MCTs to their diet may improve nutrient absorption. People often consume MCTs in supplement form as MCT oil. This supplement is available online without a prescription.

Foods to avoid with pancreatitis

Alcohol may increase the risk of chronic pancreatitis and should be avoided.

Alcohol

Drinking alcohol during an acute pancreatitis attack can worsen the condition or contribute to chronic pancreatitis. Chronic alcohol use can also cause high triglyceride levels, a major risk factor for pancreatitis. For people whose chronic pancreatitis is caused by alcohol abuse, drinking alcohol can result in severe health issues and even death.

Fried foods and high-fat foods

Fried foods and high-fat foods, such as burgers and french fries, can be problematic for people with pancreatitis. The pancreas helps with fat digestion, so foods with more fat make the pancreas work harder. Other examples of high-fat foods to avoid, include:

• dairy products

• processed meats, such as hot dogs and sausage

• mayonnaise

• potato chips

Eating these types of processed, high-fat foods can also lead to heart disease.

people with chronic pancreatitis limit their intake of refined carbohydrates, such as white bread and high sugar foods. Refined carbohydrates can lead to the pancreas releasing larger amounts of insulin. Foods that are high in sugar can also raise triglycerides. High triglyceride levels are a risk factor for acute pancreatitis.

Diet tips for recovering from pancreatitis

People recovering from pancreatitis may find that they tolerate smaller, more frequent meals. Eating six times per day may work better than eating three meals per day. A moderate fat diet, providing around 25 percent of calories from fat, may be tolerated by many people with chronic pancreatitis. people recovering from acute pancreatitis eat less than 30 grams of fat per day.

Prevention tips

Certain risk factors for pancreatitis, such as family history, cannot be changed. However, people can change some lifestyle factors that impact risk. Obesity increases the risk for pancreatitis, so achieving and maintaining a healthy weight may help lower risk of developing pancreatitis. A healthy weight also lowers risk for gallstones, which are a common cause of pancreatitis. Drinking large amounts of alcohol and smoking also raise an individual's risk for pancreatitis, so cutting back or avoiding these can help with preventing the condition.

Other treatment options

Vitamin supplements may be recommended, and the type of vitamin will depend on the individual. Treatment for pancreatitis may involve hospitalization, intravenous fluids, pain medicine, and antibiotics. A doctor may prescribe a low-fat diet, but people who are unable to eat by mouth may need an alternate way of receiving nutrition.

Surgery or other medical procedures may be recommended for some cases of pancreatitis. People with chronic pancreatitis may have difficulty digesting and absorbing certain nutrients. These issues raise the risk of the person becoming malnourished. People with chronic pancreatitis may need to take digestive enzyme pills to help with digestion and absorbing nutrients. Depending on the person, certain vitamin supplements may be recommended. Supplements may include the following:

• multivitamin

• calcium

• iron

• folate

• vitamin A

• vitamin D

• vitamin E

• vitamin K

• vitamin B-12

People should ask their healthcare provider if they should take a multivitamin. Consuming adequate amounts of fluid is also important. It is also important to speak to a healthcare provider before starting to take any supplements, such as MCT oil.

Changes to Prevent Pancreatitis Recurrence

• If you smoke cigarettes or use other tobacco products, stop.

• Eat three to four small meals each day.

• Stay hydrated; drink at least 8 ounces of water per 10 pounds of body weight each day.

• Meditate and practice relaxation to ease stress and pain.

• Practice yoga twice each week. According to a study published in the World Journal of Gastroenterology, yoga improves overall quality of life for those with chronic pancreatitis. (36)

Pancreatitis Diet Key Points

300,000 people are admitted to U.S. hospitals each year with pancreatitis. Possible complications include diabetes, malnutrition, infection, kidney failure and internal bleeding. Chronic pancreatitis is associated with a higher risk for pancreatic cancer.

Diet plays a major role in the development and treatment of pancreatitis. A pancreatitis diet features small, low-fat, nutrient-dense meals. Normalizing blood sugar levels is key to recovery.

Natural Pancreatitis Treatments

Following a Mediterranean diet is beneficial for glucose management and is associated with a lower risk of pancreatic cancer. Lean proteins, whole grains, nuts, fruits, vegetables and moderate amounts of dairy provide necessary energy and keep you satisfied. Practicing yoga twice each week is shown to improve the overall quality of life for those with chronic pancreatitis.

PANCREATITIS IN DOGS

Pancreatitis in dogs is one of those conditions that owners must be informed about before it strikes because the warning signs may not always be obvious at first, the symptoms might be mistaken for something less serious, and yet it's potentially life-threatening. The medical definition of pancreatitis is simple: "inflammation of the pancreas." But like all serious conditions, there is more to it than that.

Because it is dangerous, a suspected case of pancreatitis needs to be addressed by a veterinarian as quickly as possible and not dealt with by "DIY" treatments. As with all medical issues, even the best online resource is not a replacement for the medical guidance from your vet. Before looking at the details of pancreatitis, let's take away the "ititis" and explain the small but vital organ itself:

The pancreas is responsible for releasing enzymes that aid in digestion. When the organ is working normally, the enzymes become active only when they reach the small intestine. In a dog with pancreatitis, however, the enzymes activate when they're released, inflaming and causing damage to the pancreas and its surrounding tissue and other organs. According to the Whole Dog Journal, the enzymes can actually begin to digest the pancreas itself, which causes extreme pain to your dog.

Classic signs of pancreatitis in dogs

• Hunched back

• Repeated vomiting

• Pain or distention of the abdomen (dog appears uncomfortable or bloated)

• Diarrhea

• Loss of appetite

- Dehydration

- Weakness/lethargy

- Fever

If your dog exhibits one of these signs, and only infrequently, monitor her. But if she exhibits multiple signs at once, and repeatedly, a call to the veterinarian quickly is vital.

Causes of pancreatitis in dogs

There are a number of causes and risk factors that can bring on pancreatitis. Though often the attack appears seemingly out of the blue. Among them are:

- A high-fat diet. This is a major cause of pancreatitis, especially for a dog who gets one large helping of fatty food in one sitting

- A history of dietary indiscretion (a medical term for saying your dog will basically eat anything)

- Obesity

- Hypothyroidism (or other endocrine diseases)

- Severe blunt trauma

- Diabetes mellitus

Certain medications or other toxins

These include cholinesterase inhibitors, calcium, potassium bromide, phenobarbital, l-asparaginase, estrogen, salicylates, azathioprine, thiazide diuretics, and vinca alkaloids. There may, in some cases, be a genetic predisposition. More about those fats: Human food is especially dangerous, though even high-fat dog food may cause pancreatitis. So owner vigilance is particularly required around holidays and other festive occasions they can bring well-meaning guests who slip your buddy a fatty piece of lamb, or a tray of buttery cookies left within reach of an eager muzzle. In fact, the day after Thanksgiving is known for more than just Black Friday bargains. It's one of the busiest days of the year pancreatitis-related emergency vet visits.

Basically, if your dog is showing any signs of abdominal pain, the worst thing to do is feed him a fatty diet. This is one of many reasons that giving your dog table scraps, as tempting as it may be, is not advisable.

How does a vet diagnose pancreatitis in dogs

• Your dog's medical history

• Blood tests to measure pancreatic enzymes

• Physical examination including stomach, gums, heart, temperature

• Radiographs or ultrasound, to rule out other causes

• Fine needle aspiration of the pancreas

as with any disease, no test should be used in isolation for diagnosis, and all clinical findings should be used in conjunction to arrive at the most appropriate diagnosis.

What's the difference between acute and chronic pancreatitis

Acute Pancreatitis

An acute attack of pancreatitis means it comes on suddenly, with no previous appearance of the condition before. It can become life threatening to other organs if the inflammation spreads.

Chronic Pancreatitis

A chronic condition is one that has developed over time, slowly, and often without symptoms. This condition can result from repeated bouts of acute pancreatitis. Both acute and chronic forms can be either severe or mild, and both result in pain.

Treatment and management of pancreatitis in dogs

Treatment for pancreatitis will depend on a dog's symptoms and any abnormalities that were detected on his blood work and urinalysis. The goal is to keep the patient comfortable and support his physiological needs while giving the pancreas time to heal.

Fluid therapy and dog medications to control nausea and pain are often necessary. Your veterinarian may prescribe dog antibiotics to treat or prevent infection. Severely affected dogs may need to be hospitalized for an extended period of time and require more aggressive treatment with feeding tubes, plasma transfusion or surgery. Research has found that dogs with pancreatitis who quickly start eating dog food again have an improved prognosis. Therefore, veterinarians aggressively use anti-nausea drugs to treat vomiting in attempt to get food into dogs with pancreatitis as soon as possible. There's no fancy treatment for acute pancreatitis. First and foremost, your dog's pain must be managed, and early intervention to prevent further complications is key. The most common treatment and management options are:

• Intravenous (IV) fluid therapy in severe pancreatitis

• Vigorous monitoring of a worsening condition

• Antiemetic medication for vomiting (to prevent dehydration)

• Resting the pancreas (withholding food and water for 24 hours)

Long-term management includes:

• Vigilant monitoring of fat intake—No table scraps allowed!

• Use of a prescription diet of gastrointestinal-supportive low-fat, or ultra-low fat, food.

• Feed smaller, more frequent meals instead of one larger meal

• Have amylase and lipase levels checked by a veterinarian regularly

Supplements be used to prevent or manage pancreatitis in dogs.
It is important to reiterate that pancreatitis is a serious condition, so home remedies shouldn't be used in place of veterinary intervention. That said,

some vets believe digestive enzyme supplements with pancreatin can help some (not all) dogs by reducing the work of the pancreas and inhibiting pancreatic secretion. These come in over-the-counter strength as well as prescription strength. Fish oil may seem counterintuitive at first, because of its high fat content, but it can actually help lower blood lipid levels. Studies suggest a high level of fish oil (about 1,000 mg. per 10 pounds of body weight for dog with high lipid levels; about half that amount for dogs with normal levels) is helpful to dogs with acute pancreatitis. When supplementing with fish oil, also supplement with 5 to 10 IU of vitamin E.There have been human studies suggesting that vitamin E (with selenium), vitamin C, beta-carotene, and methionine may help prevent pancreatitis. Conversely, another human study reveals that probiotics can make acute pancreatitis worse.

Always speak with your veterinarian before offering any supplements to your pet.

Beanie, unlike most Salukis, loves to eat. But one day, after eating his very favorite treat a flaky biscuit he vomited it up. He was standing with his back kind of hunched. I gently pressed on his abdomen, and he yelped. Out came the thermometer, which told me his temperature was 103 degrees. While I was calling the veterinarian, he vomited again, then lay down in a corner. We were in the car within minutes.

The veterinarian palpated his abdomen, which was definitely tender; took his temperature, which was still high; and drew blood. Beanie received pain medication, antibiotics, and intravenous fluids to combat fluid loss and came home with strict instructions not to eat that day. Eating anything or even smelling food could have caused his pancreas to secrete enzymes and slow its healing. He could lick ice cubes, and then drink a bit of water.

The next day, he was allowed to eat about six tiny meals of low-fat, high-carbohydrate food. This meant rice, potatoes, or pasta. Overcooking these starchy foods makes them easier to digest. We would boil one cup of white rice (not instant rice) in four cups of water for 30 minutes to make a rice porridge called congee. We gradually added in protein sources, such as skinless chicken breast, low-fat cottage cheese, or boiled hamburger meat. When feeding a dog with pancreatitis, it's important to cook all the food even if you normally feed a raw diet. Because the dog's gut is compromised, it's necessary to remove fat and destroy bacteria. After a week, Beanie progressed to a veterinary prescription diet for dogs with pancreatitis. He hated it. Many dogs with a history of acute pancreatitis must be on a special diet for the rest of their lives. If they don't like the pancreatitis diet, a low-fat weight loss diet often works just as well. Since obese dogs are more prone to pancreatitis, they need to lose weight anyway. Even if a high-fat meal didn't cause the initial bout, it can trigger a recurrence once the dog has had pancreatitis.

How to Avoid Pancreatitis in Dogs

We can never completely stop pancreatitis from happening to our dogs. However, we can drastically reduce the risk of them getting one if we follow these preventive measures:

Managing Your Dog's Weight

It's crucial that you keep your dog in a healthy weight. The bigger he gets, the higher his chances of getting pancreatitis. You can manage your dog's weight by keeping a weighing scale at home, or you can also weigh him on your regular visit to the vet. For those owners who have overweight dogs, it would be great if you're going to establish an exercise routine for your dog. You can go for walks or run on the beach; anything active can already be a big help in keeping your dog at a healthy weight.

Avoiding Fatty Foods

The food is one of the biggest reasons why dogs get pancreatitis. Specifically, fatty foods are not encouraged. Thus, don't feed them table scraps be it on holidays or on regular days. Also, if you have visitors coming over, tell them not to feed your dog random foods. Sticking to a healthy diet is a must here, so ask your vet what ideal foods your dog should eat, or you can take a look at the best dog foods for pancreatitis below.

Controlling Food Portions

No matter how healthy your dog's diet is, if the portions are still big, then you and your dog will not benefit from this. That's why it's essential that you ask your vet what the ideal food portion for your dog is.

Keeping an Eye on Your Dog Outside

As mentioned above, your dog may scavenge on garbage cans, so keep an eye on him. You can either tie him on a leash or supervise his playtime outside.

Discussing the Medications Your Dog is Taking with Your Vet

Lastly, if your dog is on medication, ask your vet if the medication that your dog is taking can cause pancreatitis.

FOODS TO AVOID ON A PANCREATITIS DIET

1. Table Scraps

Did you know that more dogs suffering from pancreatitis are brought to Emergency Vet Clinics during Christmas holidays? This is because most of us cave under our pup's pleading eyes and treat them with leftovers. Our food is fattier and harder to digest for our canine companions and leads to an inflamed pancreas. So don't cave under your dog's sad pleading eyes and instead of leftovers offer him a healthy treat.

Generally speaking, your dog shouldn't be fed and treated with fatty human food leftovers. Stick with your dog's regular food in order to prevent obesity and pancreatitis.

2. High-Fat Diets

Foods that are high in fats are harder to digest and cause high levels of cortisol in the body. That's why dogs that suffer from pancreatitis should eat low fat dog food.

Diets that have from 7-10% fats are considered low fat, everything higher than that will cause a diseased pancreas to work overtime. Furthermore, fatty food will cause weight gain and obesity hence making your dog even more susceptible to develop pancreatitis. In some cases, dogs fed low fat diet can develop vitamin A and E deficiencies and can benefit from adding coconut or salmon oil into their diet. Moreover, salmon oil has proven to be beneficial in treating acute pancreatitis so you should be given it to your dog.

3. Starch

Since pancreas produces insulin, pancreatitis and diabetes are more closely related than many owners realize. So dogs with diabetes are more susceptible to pancreatitis, moreover, pancreatitis can lead to diabetes.

This means that sugar intake must be carefully monitored for dogs that are suffering from pancreatitis. Foods that have higher glycemic index are able to raise blood glucose quickly which ultimately leads to diabetes. And once a dog develops an inflamed pancreas it is best not to feed him with foods that contain a lot of sugar, like honey for example. So try to avoid vegetables that are high in sugar like pumpkin, corn, and, potatoes. Some grains like rice, oatmeal, and millet are also considered starches but if cooked a bit longer won't cause a spike in blood sugar. In fact, boiled rice with chicken breasts is recommended type of meal for dogs who have inflamed pancreas.

4. Low-quality proteins

Commercially made diets like kibble and canned food often contain low quality or unnamed protein sources. Dogs that suffer from pancreatitis shouldn't eat this types of food since some meats are fattier and harder to digest. Protein is the most important nutrient and should always be listed as the main ingredient in commercial food. If you opt for making your dog's meals at home meat needs to be a primary source and present in the right amount. If you are making your pup's food at home his pancreatitis diet should consist of skinless white chicken meat, lean and low-fat beef, beef heart, beef kidney, beef liver, and egg whites. On the other hand, if you don't have time for cooking, opt for canned or dry food that contains chicken or turkey.

5. Fillers/ Low-quality food

Even completely healthy dogs can have problems digesting fillers like wheat, soy, and corn, so dogs with pancreatitis should be kept away from them. They already lack enzymes necessary for normal digestion, and nutrients like these can cause even more trouble. In most cases, a vet will advise that a dog with pancreatitis be transitioned to a new diet. They may recommend homemade, raw, or a special high quality and low-fat pancreatitis appropriate dog food. The main thing to remember is you need to feed your dog healthy and easily digestible nutrients that won't be taxing on the pancreas.

NUTRITIONAL REQUIRMENTS

The nutritional quality of a dog's food directly affects every aspect of their life. There are several factors in determining nutritional requirement of a patient. They include the body condition scoring of the patient, the life stage of the patient and their health status. For patients diagnosed with pancreatitis, and particularly those who are admitted to hospital with acute pancreatitis, the protocol for meeting nutritional needs is compounded by the need to reduce pancreatic secretions and allow the pancreas to recover. Patients are placed on IV fluids, given anti-emetic and pain medications and fed small amounts of bland low fat food. The most important consideration in diet is that food provided is low in fat, and for the first few days they are given only about 25% of the amount they are normally fed.

Body Condition Scoring

All patients are weighed when they are admitted to hospital. This particular measurement is important because medicine doses and IV fluid rates are based on a patient's weight. In addition to a measurement in kilograms, however, an important indicator of healthy weight is the Body Score. Body score is measured on a scale of 1 to 9. Body score charts shows diagrams of five different body types, ranging from a 1/9, which is severely underweight, to a 9/9 which is obese. In general, the body condition scoring of an otherwise healthy patient will help determine whether or not that particular animal requires fewer or more calories (and other nutrients such as protein) in their diet (ie if they are severely underweight or severely overweight). Pancreatitis is more likely to occur in overweight dogs. In addition to choosing an appropriate food to control the pancreatitis, the veterinarian may suggest a diet which also limits calories. This will help to control excessive weight which can exacerbate the condition.

The Life Stage of the Patient

A dog's dietary needs change over the course of its life. Young puppies require almost four times the energy that adult dogs require and will also benefit from increased protein which helps build new tissues. At the age of 2 years (or even 1 year in the case of very small dogs) the dietary needs change and it is recommended that these dogs are given a high quality diet with:

• High quality, animal-based protein for muscle maintenance

• Fibre for a healthy digestive tract

• Essential vitamins and minerals for the immune system

• Vitamin rich fish oils for a healthy coat and skin and for overall health

• Healthy grains for energy (taken from pet Nutrition Life Stages, VPI)

Senior dogs (those who are in the last third of their life expectancy) are typically less active and so require a diet which is lower in calories, protein and fat. This is important to help prevent obesity, a common problem for older dogs. The diet for senior dogs should also be higher in fibre to enhance gastrointestinal health. As older dogs can tend to develop health problems, there are many specialized foods that can address various conditions.

Health Status

Dogs that are middle aged or older, or who are overweight, or who have a history of gastrointestinal disturbances or endocrinopathies, are considered to be at a higher risk of developing pancreatitis. There are a variety of foods available to help control a wide range of health problems. Hill's brand, for example, offers prescription diets such as z/d, u/d, t/d, and w/d to assist in the treatment of adverse food reaction, bladder health, oral health and weight control (respectively).

This report, however, will only address those foods that are appropriate for pancreatitis patients. The goal in feeding these patients is to minimize the triggering of the enzymes that cause the inflammation. As the dog begins to recover from the attack of pancreatitis small amounts of low fat, highly digestible (usually bland) foods may be introduced. For some cases, a liquid food might be the first oral food introduced.

Once the patient is tolerating the liquid food, dogs can be placed on a low fat, high fibre diet. "…moderate fiber diets, containing 10–15% dry matter, and moderate fat contents (10–15%)…." can be fed. Carbohydrates have a weak effect on the hormones which trigger pancreatic enzymes and they aid digestion. Rice is a commonly used ingredient in both commercial and homemade diets for pancreatic patients. Boiled chicken, low fat beef, egg whites, yogurt, barley and cooked vegetables are also considered safe foods for pancreatitis patients.

FOOD COMPARISONS

Owners have several choices of types of foods when feeding a pet with pancreatitis. A wide range of commercial foods are available, from budget supermarket brands to premium foods to prescription foods. Alternatively, owners might choose to make their own food at home. Homemade foods may fall within the category of raw food (ie: the BARF diet) or cooked food.

Commercial Foods (Supermarket and Premium). While many manufacturers advertise their product as being complete and balanced, there is a clear difference in the content of foods across the broad range of what is available to purchase. Premium brands contain a higher quality of food and so will have a higher nutrient content.

Prescription Foods

Prescription foods that veterinarians might recommend specifically for dogs with gastrointestinal problems such as pancreatitis are: Hill's Prescription Diet i/d or Royal Canin Gastrointestinal Low Fat. It is generally recommended that the food for pancreatitis patients should contain less than 18% fat. Some veterinarians recommend that the fat content be less than 8%. Hill's i/d contains 14.9% fat while the Royal Canin contains 7% fat.

Homemade Foods

Another alternative available to pet owners is to make their pet's food themselves. While a drawback to this choice is that the process is time consuming, some pet owners are happier with this as they feel they know exactly what their pet is eating, that they can provide a safer, more natural diet and, in some cases, create a diet more suited to their philosophical views, choosing vegetarian, organic or raw diets. "A recent survey reports that 10% of owners feed a non-commercial diet to provide 50% or more of their pet's intake."(from Home Cooked vs Commercial diets). While the internet abounds with websites offering recipes for homemade dog food, most cannot guarantee the percentage of protein, fat or vitamins contained in the food. If an owner is keen to prepare their own food, we recommend seeking the services of a veterinary nutritionist. Massey University in New Zealand has an excellent service.

Typically, the cost for 'special' foods is higher than the cost for 'normal' foods. This is true whether you choose commercial, prescription or homemade foods and supplements. The table below outlines the cost comparisons between two premium brands available at most veterinary practices, and the cheaper, supermarket brands. Included as well are costs for both animal grade and human grade meats that can make up a homemade diet.

POTENTIAL ADVERSE REACTIONS

It is true that commercially processed dog foods are vastly different from the foods that dogs would eat in the wild. Dogs in the wild eat not only the meat of their prey, but consume as well the bone, intestines, and organs like the liver. All these are a source of important nutrients. Diligent pet owners and manufacturers of commercial pet food are all interested in creating a food that not only replicates the wild dogs' food, but improves upon it for domesticated dogs. We also hope to support our dog's lives for longer than 6-8 years, the average age of a wolf. This is not an easy task. There is much competition between manufacturers. The combination of their advertising and the increasing prevalence of on-line forums about canine diets can leave the average consumer reeling with confusion.

There is no Australian standard for dry or processed pet food. There is, however, an Australian standard for frozen and fresh pet meat, which was generated by the Primary Industry Ministerial Council's Meat Standards Committee. It is enforced by the state's controlling authorities. The standard covers all stages of the pet meat production process to ensure:

• It remains separate to human-grade meat.

• Is hygienically handled.

• Is free from harmful diseases.

So while owners may feel assured that the meat they purchase has met certain standards at point of sale, there are still a number of risks to take into account when they endeavor to make their pet's food at home. "If raw animal products are included (such as meat, eggs, organs), concerns regarding contamination with pathogenic microorganisms should be discussed with the owner, particularly if vulnerable family members or others have contact with the animal or its feces (i.e., infants, elderly, immunocompromised)."(taken from Home Cooked vs Commercial diets). Additionally, any other potentially dangerous ingredients should be identified (i.e., grapes/raisins, garlic/onions, bones). There is the potential for whole bones to choke an animal, break teeth or cause an internal puncture. Further, there is a chance that the owner may not choose the appropriate ingredients (based on advice they may receive from a number of people, not the least of which are sources on the internet). They could inadvertently create an unbalanced diet that, if continued over a long period of time, may actually damage their dog's health. With regard to the claims made by commercial manufacturers about "low fat' foods, there can be adverse reactions if a dog is fed a diet that is too low in fat. "Diets that are too low in fat can lead to deficiencies of fat-soluble vitamins and problems with the skin and coat; they can also leave your dog feeling tired and hungry all the time."(Taken from 'Healthy Low-Fat Diets For Dogs With Special Dietary Needs'

Other considerations include:

• allergies or food intolerance to the protein source (e.g. chicken) Usually other options are available such as fish or beef based, but one cannot be sure of fat content.

• Processing contamination potentially causing toxicity. A possible result could be liver failure, something unlikely in commercial diets

• Poisoning in home cooked diets (eg salmonella). This is entirely possible as the owner may make up a large quality and it might go off. The owner might also have a tendency to by meat on 'special' which usually has a short use by date.

ADVICE FOR OWNERS

The best advice for owners is to discuss their pet's dietary needs with their veterinarian. Typically a pancreatitis patient is discharged with fairly standard advice on diet: feed a low fat, high fibre diet and keep the caloric content low. For the veterinarians who work at a general practice where premium dog food is sold, the owner can be directed to purchase a premium food, such as Hil's i/d or Royal Canin Veterinary Diet Digestive Low Fat. If the owner wishes to make their own dog food, then they should be advised to focus on low fat meats such as low fat chicken breast. Meats high in fat such as lamb and pork should be avoided. Rice is a commonly used ingredient in homemade diets for pancreatic patients. Other ingredients include low fat beef, beef organs (kidney, heart, liver), egg whites, yogurt, barley and cooked vegetables.

If the veterinarian advises to feed a homecooked meal, they must provide a specific diet plan so as not to inadvertently cause to owner to feed their pet a non-balance diet. We would recommend to our clients that that most convenient, accurate and economical option is to feed a commercially prepared prescription diet specifically formulated to meet their pet's requirements. It is also advisable to give their dog several small meals in a day rather than one large one. This is particularly important to ease the process of digestion.

Dietary management and prevention

Getting the diet right is absolutely crucial for managing chronic pancreatitis and preventing future acute episodes. Please note that these guidelines are meant for adult maintenance only, not for puppies or females who are pregnant or nursing, as their requirements are different.

The aim should be to reduce the workload on the pancreas as much as possible so you should aim for a diet that is Low in fat (between 5% and 10% dry matter). Highly digestible (good quality and free from any potentially problematic ingredients). And, as an added precaution, we also recommend looking for Moderate protein (between 20% and 30% dry matter). Not too starchy (avoid foods with large amounts of starchy ingredients like maize, white potato, white rice, tapioca, pea starch etc)

No added sugars

Suggested Dog Food Directory filters for a dog with pancreatitis Commercial dog foods

That's all well and good, I hear you cry, but how on earth am I going to find a food matching those criteria? Well, you can either ask your favourite dog food manufacturer if they have something suitable or you can use the filters in our Dog Food Directory to get a list of all the foods that might fit the bill. As well as entering your dog's details and your budget, we would recommend using the filters shown in the picture for dogs that are prone to pancreatitis. Our product ratings are designed to indicate how healthy a food is likely to be for the majority of dogs and encompasses factors like the suitability and quality of ingredients so once you have the list of suitable foods, it is always best to first look at the ones with the best ratings. Do remember to introduce the new food into the diet slowly. This will help the system to adjust gradually and will make it easier for you to spot and rectify any potential issues early on.

Home-prepared food

A suitable home prepared diet, be it cooked or raw, can work wonders for dogs with digestive problems like pancreatitis but careful planning is crucial. The points above are a good place to start but to fully cover recipe formulation for pancreatitic dogs is, frankly, an article in itself which will have to go on to the to-do list for now. In the meantime, though, this page provides a fairly comprehensive guide on the subject.

Treats for dogs with pancreatitisTreats, leftovers and tidbits

Be sure to avoid any treats, tidbits and table scraps that are high in fat or of a low quality - the Treat Directory will help you to find suitable alternatives. Make sure other family members and friends are also onboard with this as even a slight indiscretion cold result in another bout of pancreatitis. It is also important to make sure your bins and pet food storage containers are well and truly dog-proof.

Supplements

Certain supplements may also help reduce the risk of acute pancreatitis or control the effects of chronic pancreatitis. You might be able to find them included in complete foods or you can add them to your dog's diet yourself. Pancreatic digestive enzyme supplements have been reported to help some dogs with pancreatitis while fish body oils (such as salmon oil or EPA oil but not cod liver oil), can help to lower blood lipid levels which may reduce the workload on the pancreas. Probiotics and prebiotics can help with digestion and may aid in the management of pancreatitis. The most common prebiotics in pet food include Mannan-oligosaccharides (MOS), fructo-oligosaccharides (FOS), inulin and chicory extract.

How long can a dog live with pancreatitis

Life expectancy for dogs diagnosed with pancreatitis is difficult to predict. In mild, uncomplicated cases, the prognosis is usually good, with most patients going on to make a full recovery. This is especially the case if high-fat diets are avoided and good veterinary and nursing care is provided. But in more serious cases the prognosis is guarded. This is partly because dogs with severe pancreatitis often have frequent acute episodes or complicating factors such as hypothermia, acidosis, hypocalcemia, and single or multiple-organ failure

CONCLUSION

Acute pancreatitis is frequently encountered on the emergency surgical take. Once the diagnosis is made, clinical efforts should simultaneously concentrate on investigating for the underlying etiology and managing the condition by anticipating its complications, which can be aided by using any of the severity scoring systems described. Management of acute pancreatitis is largely supportive. There is still no consensus on the ideal type and regimen of fluid for resuscitation, but goal-directed fluid therapy is associated with better outcomes. Early enteral nutrition modulates the inflammatory response and improves outcomes by decreasing infective complications of acute pancreatitis. Antibiotics should be used judiciously as prophylactic antibiotics have not shown any benefit in preventing infective complications of acute pancreatitis. Patients with mild acute gallstone pancreatitis should be recommended to undergo a laparoscopic cholecystectomy at the index admission, while those with severe gallstone pancreatitis and evidence of cholangitis and/or choledocholithiasis benefit from early ERCP. Patients with mild acute gallstone pancreatitis and concurrent choledocholithiasis benefit from single-stage laparoscopic cholecystectomy and bile duct exploration, subject to available local expertise. There is no difference in mortality and morbidity between the single-stage and double-stage management of choledocholithiasis. However, the single-stage approach reduces the length of hospital stay and need for recurrent admissions.